Abbreviations and Symbols

beg .... begin(ning)
bl(s) .... back loop(s)
ch(s) .... chain(s)
dc .... double crochet(s)
dec .... decrease(-ing)
dtrc .... double triple crochet(s)
FPdc ...... front post double crochet(s)
hdc .... half double crochet(s)
lp(s) .... loop(s)
patt .... pattern
prev .... previous
rem .... remain(ing)
rep .... repeat(ing)
rnd(s) .... round(s)
sc .... single crochet(s)
sk .... skip
sl .... slip
sl st(s) .... slip stitch(es)
sp(s) .... space(s)
st(s) .... stitch(es)
tog .... together
trc .... triple crochet(s)
tr trc .... triple triple crochet(s)
YO .... yarn over

* An asterisk is used to mark the beginning of a portion of instructions which will be worked more than once; thus, "rep from * twice" means after working the instructions once, repeat the instructions following the asterisk twice more (3 times in all).

† The dagger identifies a portion of instructions that will be repeated again later in the same row or round.

: The number after a colon at the end of a row indicates the number of stitches you should have when the row has been completed.

() Parentheses are used to enclose instructions which should be worked the exact number of times specified immediately following the parentheses, such as (2 sc in next dc, sc in next dc) twice. They are also used to set off and clarify a group of stitches that are to be worked all into the same space or stitch, such as (2 dc, ch 1, 2 dc) in corner sp.

[] Brackets and () parentheses are used to provide additional information to clarify instructions.

Join - join with a sl st unless otherwise specified.

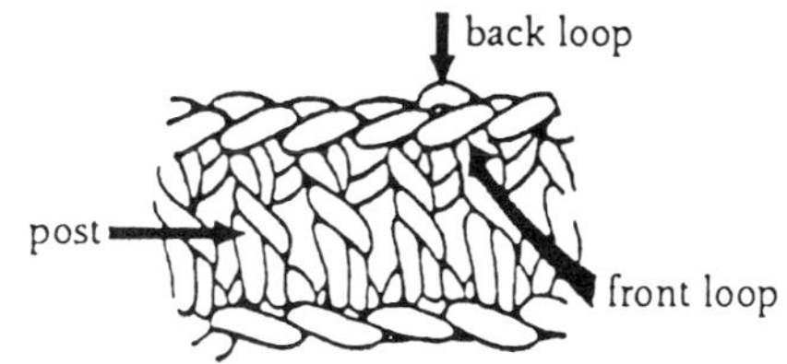

Front loop is the loop toward you at the top of the stitch.
Back loop is the loop away from you at the top to the stitch.
Post is the part of the stitch around which a front post stitch is worked.

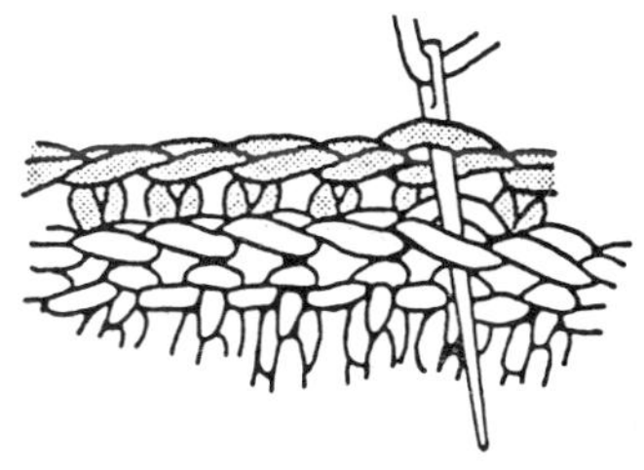

Overcast stitch is worked loosely.

The patterns in this book are written using United States terminology. Terms which have different English equivalents are noted below.

United States	English	United States	English
single crochet (sc)	double crochet(dc)	skip (sk)	miss
half double crochet (hdc)	half treble (htr)	slip stitch (sl st)	slip stitch (ss) (or "single crochet")
double crochet (dc)	treble (tr)	yarn over (YO)	yarn over hook (YOH)
triple crochet (trc)	double treble (dtr)	gauge	tension
triple triple crochet (tr trc)	quadruple treble [q(uad) tr]	worsted weight yarn	double knitting weight

Metric Conversion Charts

INCHES INTO MILLIMETERS AND CENTIMETERS *(Rounded off slightly)*

inches	mm	cm	inches	cm	inches	cm	inches	cm
1/8	3		5	12.5	21	53.5	38	96.5
1/4	6		5½	14	22	56	39	99
3/8	10	1	6	15	23	58.5	40	101.5
1/2	13	1.3	7	18	24	61	41	104
5/8	15	1.5	8	20.5	25	63.5	42	106.5
3/4	20	2	9	23	26	66	43	109
7/8	22	2.2	10	25.5	27	68.5	44	112
1	25	2.5	11	28	28	71	45	114.5
1¼	32	3.2	12	30.5	29	73.5	46	117
1½	38	3.8	13	33	30	76	47	119.5
1¾	45	4.5	14	35.5	31	79	48	122
2	50	5	15	38	32	81.5	49	124.5
2½	65	6.5	16	40.5	33	84	50	127
3	75	7.5	17	43	34	86.5		
3½	90	9	18	46	35	89		
4	100	10	19	48.5	36	91.5		
4½	115	11.5	20	51	37	94		

mm — millimeter cm — centimeters

CROCHET HOOKS CONVERSION CHART										
U.S.	1/B	2/C	3/D	4/E	5/F	6/G	8/H	9/I	10/J	10½/K
English	12	11	10	9	8	7	6	5	4	2
Continental—m.m.	2.25	2.75	3.25	3.5	3.75	4.25	5	5.5	6	6.5

A Word About Yarns

The soft look and feel of the afghans in this book can be achieved by using a soft acrylic worsted weight yarn such as Bouquet Softee, Caron Gold™, or Aunt Lydia's®. Other worsted weight yarns may be used, but the completed afghan may not have the same look.

Victorian Vineyard

SIZE:

About 40" x 60" before tassel fringe

MATERIALS:

Worsted weight yarn (see A Word About Yarns, page 2), 60 oz (4200 yds) lavender

Size F aluminum crochet hook, or size required for gauge

GAUGE:

(5 puff sts, dc) twice = 5 1/2"

PATTERN STITCH

PUFF STITCH

YO, insert hook in next ch or st, draw up lp; (YO, insert hook in same ch or st, draw up lp) 3 times; YO and draw through all 9 lps on hook: puff st made.

Instructions

Ch 229 loosely.

Row 1 (right side)**:** Dc in 4th ch from hook (3 skipped chs count as a dc), * ch 3, sk next 3 chs, puff st (see Patten Stitch above) in next ch, (ch 1, sk next ch, puff st in next ch) 4 times; ch 3, sk next 3 chs, dc in next ch; rep from * 13 times more; dc in next ch: fourteen 5-puff st groups; ch 4 (counts as first dc and ch-1 sp on following rows), turn.

Row 2: Dc in next dc, * † ch 3, sk next puff st, puff st in next ch, (ch 1, sk next puff st, puff st in next ch) 3 times; ch 3, sk next puff st and next 2 chs, dc in next ch, ch 1 †, sk next dc, dc in next ch; rep from * 12 times more, then rep from † to † once; sk next dc, dc in next dc: fourteen 4-puff st groups; ch 3 (counts as first dc on following rows), turn.

Row 3: Dc in next ch, ch 1, dc in next dc, ch 3, * † sk next puff st, puff st in next ch, (ch 1, sk next puff st, puff st in next ch) twice; ch 3, sk next puff st and next 2 chs, dc in next ch †, (ch 1, sk next dc, dc in next ch) twice; ch 3; rep from * 12 times more, then rep from † to † once; ch 1, sk next dc, dc in next ch, dc in next dc: fourteen 3-puff st groups; ch 4, turn.

Row 4: Sk next dc, dc in next ch, ch 1, sk next dc, dc in next ch, ch 3, * † sk next puff st, puff st in next ch, ch 1, puff st in next ch, ch 3, sk next puff st and next 2 chs, dc in next ch †, (ch 1, sk next dc, dc in next ch) 3 times; ch 3; rep from * 12 times more, then rep from † to † once; ch 1, sk next dc, dc in next ch, ch 1, sk next dc, dc in next dc: fourteen 2-puff st groups; ch 3, turn.

Row 5: Dc in next ch, (ch 1, sk next dc, dc in next ch) twice; ch 3, * † sk next puff st, dc in next ch, ch 3, sk next puff st and next 2 chs, dc in next ch †, (ch 1, sk next dc, dc in next ch) 4 times; ch 3; rep from * 12 times more, then rep from † to † once; (ch 1, sk next dc, dc in next ch) twice; dc in next dc; ch 4, turn.

Row 6: Sk next dc, dc in next ch, ch 1, sk next dc, dc in next ch, * † ch 3, sk next dc and next 2 chs, puff st in next ch, ch 1, sk next dc, puff st in next ch, ch 3, sk next dc, dc in next ch †, (ch 1, sk next dc, dc in next ch) 3 times; rep from * 12 times more, then rep from † to † once; ch 1, sk next dc, dc in next ch, ch 1, sk next dc, dc in next dc: fourteen 2-puff st groups; ch 3, turn.

Row 7: Dc in next ch, ch 1, sk next dc, dc in next ch, ch 3, * † sk next dc and next 2 chs, puff st in next ch, (ch 1, sk next puff st, puff st in next ch) twice; ch 3, sk next dc, dc in next ch †, (ch 1, sk next dc, dc in next ch) twice; ch 3; rep from * 12 times more, then rep from † to † once; ch 1, sk next dc, dc in next ch and in next dc: fourteen 3-puff st groups; ch 4, turn.

Row 8: Sk next dc, dc in next ch, ch 3, * † sk next dc and next 2 chs, puff st in next ch, (ch 1, sk next puff st, puff st

(continued)

in next ch) 3 times; ch 3, sk next dc, dc in next ch, ch 1, sk next dc †, dc in next ch, ch 3; rep from * 12 times more, then rep from † to † once; dc in next dc: fourteen 4-puff st groups; ch 3, turn.

Row 9: Dc in next ch, ch 3, * † sk next dc and next 2 chs, puff st in next ch, (ch 1, sk next puff st, puff st in next ch) 4 times; ch 3, sk next 2 chs and next dc, dc in next ch †, ch 3; rep from * 12 times more, then rep from † to † once; dc in next dc: fourteen 5-puff st groups; ch 4, turn.

Row 10: Sk next dc, dc in next ch, ch 3, * † sk next puff st, puff st in next ch, (ch 1, sk next puff st, puff st in next ch) 3 times; ch 3, sk next puff st and next 2 chs, dc in next ch, ch 1, sk next dc †, dc in next ch, ch 3; rep from * 12 times more, then rep from † to † once; dc in next dc: fourteen 4-puff st groups; ch 3, turn.

Rep Rows 3 through 10 until afghan measures about 56".

Rep Rows 3 through 9 once. At end of Row 9, ch 1, turn.

SIDE EDGINGS:

Ch 1, working along side edge in lps formed by turning chs, 2 sc in each lp. Finish off.

Hold afghan with right side facing you and other side edge at top; join yarn in right-hand corner. Working across side edge, work same as prev side edging. Weave in all ends.

TASSEL FRINGE (make 28)

Cut twenty-six 32" strands of yarn for one tassel. Using crochet hook, pull 5 strands through each puff st of first 5-puff st group on one short end of afghan; adjust strands so ends are even. Referring to photo, wrap remaining strand loosely around all 25 doubled strands, about 1 1/2" from edge of afghan, wrapping 9 times and knotting at back of tassel. Repeat for tassel in each 5-puff st group across each short end of afghan. Trim ends evenly.

Carriage Wheels

SIZE:

About 40" x 54" without border

MATERIALS:

Worsted weight yarn (see A Word About Yarns, page 2), 40 oz (2800 yds) peach

Size F aluminum crochet hook, or size required for gauge

15 yds 1/4"-wide peach satin ribbon

GAUGE:

(shell, V-st) twice = 4 1/2"

12 patt rows = 4 1/2"

Instructions

CENTER

Ch 194 loosely.

Row 1 (right side)**:** Sc in 2nd ch from hook, * ch 3, sk next 5 chs, in next ch work [dc, (ch 1, dc) 4 times]: shell made; ch 3, sk next 5 chs, sc in next ch; rep from * 15 times more: 16 shells; ch 3 (counts as first dc on following rows), turn.

Row 2: Dc in first sc, * † ch 1, sk next dc, sc in next ch-1 sp, (ch 3, sc in next ch-1 sp) 3 times; ch 1 †, in next sc work (dc, ch 2, dc): V-st made; rep from * 14 times more, then rep from † to † once; 2 dc in next sc; ch 3, turn.

Row 3: Dc between next 2 dc, * † ch 2, sc in next ch-3 lp, (ch 3, sc in next ch-3 lp) twice; ch 2 †, V-st in ch-2 sp of next V-st: V-st in V-st made; rep from * 14 times more, then rep from † to † once; dc between next 2 dc, dc in next dc; ch 3, turn.

Row 4: Dc between next 2 dc, * † ch 3, (sc in next ch-3 lp, ch 3) twice †; V-st in next V-st; rep from * 14 times more, then rep from † to † once; dc between next 2 dc, dc in next dc; ch 3, turn.

Row 5: Dc between next 2 dc, * † ch 1, sk next ch-3 lp, shell in next ch-3 lp, ch 1 †, V-st in next V-st; rep from * 14 times more, then rep from † to † once; dc between next 2 dc, dc in next dc; ch 3, turn.

Row 6: Dc between next 2 dc, * † ch 1, sk next ch-1 sp, sc in next ch-1 sp, (ch 3, sc in next ch-1 sp) 3 times; ch 1 †, V-st in next V-st; rep from * 14 times more, then rep from † to † once; dc between next 2 dc, dc in next dc; ch 3, turn.

Rep Rows 3 through 6 until Center measures about 53".

Rep Rows 3 and 4 once. At end of Row 4, ch 1, turn.

EDGING:

Rnd 1: Work 150 sc evenly spaced across top edge; work 200 sc evenly spaced across next side; work 150 sc evenly spaced across lower edge; work 200 sc evenly spaced across next side; join in first sc: 700 sc.

Rnd 2: Ch 4 (counts as a dc and ch-1 sp), in same sc as joining work (dc, ch 1, dc); ch 1, † sk next sc, (dc in next sc, ch 1, sk next sc) 74 times; in next sc work (dc, ch 1, dc, ch 1, dc); ch 1, sk next sc, (dc in next sc, ch 1, sk next sc) 99 times †; in next sc work (dc, ch 1, dc, ch 1, dc); ch 1; rep from † to † once; join in 3rd ch of beg ch-4. Finish off and weave in ends.

BORDER

FIRST MOTIF:

Ch 4.

Row 1 (right side)**:** 8 dc in 4th ch from hook (3 skipped chs count as a dc): 9 dc; ch 5, turn.

Row 2: Sk next dc, dc in next dc, (ch 2, sk next dc, dc in next dc) 3 times; ch 1, turn.

Row 3: Sc in next dc, * in next ch-2 sp work (sc, ch 4, sc), sc in next dc; rep from * twice more; in turning ch-5 lp work (sc, ch 4, sc), sc in 3rd ch of same ch-5 lp; ch 12

(counts as first trc and ch-8 lp on following row), turn.

Row 4: * Sk next sc, next ch-4 lp, and next sc; trc in next sc, ch 8; rep from * twice more; sk next sc, next ch-4 lp, and next sc; trc in next sc; ch 1, turn.

Row 5: Sc in next trc, 10 sc in next ch-8 lp: base of pineapple made; ch 1, turn, leaving rem sts unworked.

Row 6: Sc in next sc, (ch 3, sk next sc, sc in next sc) 5 times; turn.

Row 7: Sl st in next ch-3 lp; ch 1, sc in same lp; (ch 3, sc in next ch-3 lp) 4 times; turn.

Row 8: Sl st in next ch-3 lp; ch 1, sc in same lp; (ch 3, sc in next ch-3 lp) 3 times; turn.

Row 9: Sl st in next ch-3 lp; ch 1, sc in same lp; (ch 3, sc in next ch-3 lp) twice; turn.

Row 10: Sl st in next ch-3 lp; ch 1, sc in same lp; ch 3, sc in next ch-3 lp; turn.

Row 11: Sk next sc, sl st in next 2 chs; ch 3, sc in next sc, working along side, (ch 3, sc in side of next row) 4 times.

Row 12: Sc in next trc, 10 sc in next ch-8 lp; ch 1, turn.

Rep Rows 6 through 12 twice more, then rep Rows 6 through 11 once. At end of last row, sc in last trc; ch 16

(continued)

(counts as first tr trc and ch-10 lp on following row), turn.

Row 13: Sc in ch-3 lp at top of next pineapple, ch 10, * tr trc in first sc of Row 5 ***between pineapples*** [to work tr trc: YO 4 times, insert hook in st and draw up lp, (YO, draw through 2 lps on hook) 5 times: tr trc made]; ch 10, sc in ch-3 lp at top of next pineapple, ch 10; rep from * twice more; tr trc in last sc; ch 1, turn.

Row 14: * Sc in next tr trc, 13 sc in next ch-10 lp, sc in next sc, 13 sc in next ch-10 lp; rep from * 3 times more; sc in 6th ch of turning ch-16; ch 1, turn.

Row 15: Sc in next sc, (ch 8, sk next 6 sc, sc in next sc) 16 times; ch 1, turn.

Row 16: Sk next sc, 10 sc in next ch-8 lp, sk next sc, * 2 sc in next ch-8 lp, ch 5, turn; sk first 4 sc, sl st in next sc; ch 1, turn; in next ch-5 lp work (3 sc; ch 4, sl st in top of last sc made: picot made; 3 sc), 8 sc in same ch-8 lp; rep from * 14 times more; join in first sc. Finish off.

SECOND MOTIF:
Ch 4.

Rows 1 through 15: Rep Rows 1 through 15 of First Motif.

Row 16: Work same as Row 16 of First Motif to last picot; ch 3, with wrong side of completed motif facing you, sl st in corresponding picot of completed motif; ch 2, sl st in top of last sc made; 3 sc in same ch-5 lp, 8 sc in same ch-8 lp; join in first sc of Row 15, ch 12; with right side of completed motif facing you, join in first sc of Row 16 on completed motif. Finish off.

Rep Second Motif 11 times more.

LAST MOTIF:
Ch 4.

Rows 1 through 15: Rep Rows 1 through 15 of First Motif.

Row 16: Sk next sc, 10 sc in next ch-8 lp, sk next sc, 2 sc in next ch-8 lp; ch 5, turn; sk first 4 sc, sl st in next sc; ch 1, turn; in next ch-5 lp work (3 sc, ch 3, sl st in top of last picot of First Motif; ch 2, sl st in last sc made; 3 sc); sk next sc, * † 8 sc in same ch-8 lp; 2 sc in next ch-8 lp, ch 5, turn, sk next 4 sc, sl st in next sc; ch 1, turn; 3 sc in next ch-5 lp †; ch 4, picot, 3 sc in same ch-5 lp; rep from * 12 times more, then rep from † to † once; ch 3, sl st in first picot of 13th motif; ch 2, sl st in last sc made; 3 sc in same ch-5 lp, 8 sc in same ch-8 lp; join in first sc of Row 15; ch 12, with right side of 13th motif facing you, join in first sc of 13th motif. Finish off.

With wrong side of First Motif facing you, join yarn in last sc of Row 16 of First Motif; ch 12, turn work so that right side is facing you, join in first sc on Row 16 of Last Motif; do not finish off, ch 1, turn.

EDGING:
* Working over chs, work 50 sc evenly spaced across each of next 3 motifs, work 54 sc evenly spaced across next motif; work 50 sc evenly spaced across each of next 2 motifs; work 54 sc evenly spaced across next motif; rep from * once more; join in first sc: 716 sc. Finish off and weave in ends.

FINISHING

With right sides together, pin joined motifs to Center, having 3 motifs along each short end and 4 motifs along each side. Sew together with overcast stitch (see page 1), working through both loops of motifs and back loop of edging.

Referring to photo for placement, weave ribbon through one side of border, leaving 12" length at each end. Repeat on remaining sides. Tie ends in bows at each corner.

Katerina

SIZE:

About 50" x 70"

MATERIALS:

Worsted weight yarn (see A Word About Yarns, page 2), 54 oz (3780 yds) rose

Size F aluminum crochet hook, or size required for gauge

GAUGE:

(shell, pineapple, shell) = 4 1/2"

7 rows = 4"

PATTERN STITCH

FRONT POST DOUBLE CROCHET (FPdc)

YO, insert hook from front to back to front around post of next st (see page 1); YO and draw lp through (3 lps on hook); (YO and draw through 2 lps on hook) twice: FPdc made.

Instructions

CENTER

Ch 184 loosely.

Row 1 (right side): 2 dc in 4th ch from hook (3 skipped chs count as a dc); * † ch 7, sk next 5 chs, sc in next ch, ch 3, sk next 2 chs, sc in next ch, ch 7, sk next 5 chs †, in next ch work (2 dc, ch 1, 2 dc): shell made; rep from * 10 times more, then rep from † to † once; 3 dc in next ch: 11 shells; ch 3 (counts as first dc on following rows), turn.

Row 2: 2 dc in first dc, ch 3, sc in next ch-7 lp, ch 5, sc in next ch-7 lp, ch 3, * in ch-1 sp of next shell work shell: shell in shell made; ch 3, sc in next ch-7 lp, ch 5, sc in next ch-7 lp, ch 3; rep from * 10 times more; sk next 2 dc, 3 dc in next dc; ch 3, turn.

Row 3: 2 dc in first dc, 11 trc in next ch-5 lp: base of pineapple made; * shell in next shell, 11 trc in next ch-5 lp: base of pineapple made; rep from * 10 times more; sk next 2 dc, 3 dc in next dc: 12 pineapple bases; ch 3, turn.

Row 4: 2 dc in first dc, ch 2, * † sc in next trc, (ch 3, sk next trc, sc in next trc) 5 times; ch 2 †, shell in next shell, ch 2; rep from * 10 times more, then rep from † to † once; sk next 2 dc, 3 dc in next dc; ch 3, turn.

Row 5: 2 dc in first dc, * † (ch 3, sc in next ch-3 lp) 5 times; ch 3 †, shell in next shell; rep from * 10 times more, then rep from † to † once; sk next 2 dc, 3 dc in next dc; ch 3, turn.

Row 6: 2 dc in first dc, * † ch 4, sk next ch-3 lp, sc in next ch-3 lp, (ch 3, sc in next ch-3 lp) 3 times; ch 4 †, shell in next shell; rep from * 10 times more, then rep from † to † once; sk next 2 dc, 3 dc in next dc; ch 3, turn.

Row 7: 2 dc in first dc, * † ch 5, sc in next ch-3 lp, (ch 3, sc in next ch-3 lp) twice; ch 5 †, shell in next shell; rep from * 10 times more, then rep from † to † once; sk next 2 dc, 3 dc in next dc; ch 3, turn.

Row 8: 2 dc in first dc, * † ch 7, sc in next ch-3 lp, ch 3, sc in next ch-3 lp, ch 7 †, shell in next shell; rep from * 10 times more, then rep from † to † once; sk next 2 dc, 3 dc in next dc; ch 3, turn.

Rep Rows 2 through 8 until Center measures about 60".

Rep Row 2 once. At end of Row 2, do not ch 3; ch 1, turn.

BORDER

Note: Border is worked in rnds.

Rnd 1: 3 sc in first sc: corner made; work 181 sc evenly spaced across top edge, 3 sc in next corner st: corner made; work 241 sc evenly spaced along next side, 3 sc in next corner st: corner made; work 181 sc evenly spaced across lower edge, 3 sc in next corner st: corner made;

(continued)

work 241 sc evenly spaced along next side; join in first sc: 856 sc.

Rnd 2: Sl st in next sc; ch 3 (counts as a dc on this and following rnds), in same sc work (dc, ch 2, 2 dc): beg corner made; sk next sc, dc in next sc, sk next sc, * † in next sc work (2 dc, ch 2, 2 dc), sk next sc, dc in next sc, sk next sc †; rep from † to † across to 2nd sc of next corner; in 2nd sc work (2 dc, ch 2, 2 dc): corner made; sk next sc, dc in next sc, sk next sc; rep from * twice more, then rep from † to † across next side; join in 3rd ch of beg ch-3.

Rnd 3: Sl st in next dc and in next ch-2 sp; ch 3, in same sp work (dc, ch 2, 2 dc); sk next 2 dc, FPdc (see Pattern Stitch on page 9) around next dc, * in next ch-2 sp work (2 dc, ch 2, 2 dc), sk next 2 dc, FPdc around next dc; rep from * around; join in 3rd ch of beg ch-3.

Rnd 4: Sl st in next dc and in next ch-2 sp; ch 3, in same sp work (dc, ch 2, 2 dc); FPdc around next FPdc, * in next ch-2 sp work (2 dc, ch 2, 2 dc), FPdc around next FPdc; rep from * around; join in 3rd ch of beg ch-3.

Rnds 5 through 8: Rep Rnd 4.

Rnd 9: Sl st in next dc and in next ch-2 sp; ch 3, 4 dc in same sp; FPdc around next FPdc, * 5 dc in next ch-2 sp, FPdc around next FPdc; rep from * around; join in 3rd ch of beg ch-3. Finish off and weave in ends.

Antique Fans

SIZE:

About 45" x 60"

MATERIALS:

Worsted weight yarn (see A Word About Yarns, page 2), 50 oz (3500 yds) green

Size G aluminum crochet hook, or size required for gauge

GAUGE:

2 fans = 6"

PATTERN STITCH

DOUBLE TRIPLE CROCHET (dtrc):

YO 3 times, insert hook in st, YO, draw lp through: 5 lps on hook; (YO, draw through 2 lps on hook) 4 times: dtrc made.

Instructions

CENTER

Ch 194 loosely.

Row 1 (right side): Sc in 2nd ch from hook, * sk next 5 chs, 13 dtrc (see Pattern Stitch above) in next ch: fan made; sk next 5 chs, sc in next ch; rep from * 15 times more: 16 fans; ch 6 (counts as first dtrc and ch-1 sp on following rows), turn.

Row 2: Dtrc in next sc, * ch 4, sc in 7th dtrc of next fan, ch 4, in next sc work (dtrc, ch 1, dtrc); rep from * 15 times more; ch 1, turn.

Row 3: Sc in next dtrc, * fan in next sc, sk next ch-4 lp and next dtrc, sc in next ch; rep from * 15 times more; ch 6, turn.

Rep Rows 2 and 3 until Center measures about 56", ending with a Row 2. At end of last row, do not ch 1; ch 5 (counts as a dtrc on following rnd), turn.

BORDER:

Rnd 1: Dtrc in next ch-1 sp, dtrc in each dtrc and in each ch across to last ch; in next ch work (dtrc, ch 12, dtrc): corner made; work 263 dtrc evenly spaced along next side to next corner; in next corner work (dtrc, ch 12, dtrc): corner made; working in unused lps of beg ch, work 191 dtrc evenly spaced to next corner; in next corner work (dtrc, ch 12, dtrc): corner made; work 263 dtrc evenly spaced along next side to corner; dtrc in same st as turning ch-5 made, ch 12; join in 5th ch of turning ch-5: 916 dtrc.

Rnd 2: Ch 1, sc in same ch as joining; * † sk next 5 dtrc, fan in next dtrc, sk next 5 dtrc, sc in next dtrc †; rep from † to † to next corner lp; ch 10, in corner ch-12 lp work (sc, ch 6, sc): corner made; ch 10, sc in next dtrc; rep from * 3 times more, ending last rep without working last sc; join in first sc: 76 fans. Finish off and weave in ends.

Anastasia

SIZE:

About 56" x 56"

MATERIALS:

Worsted weight yarn (see A Word About Yarns, page 2), 57 oz (3990 yds) off-white

Size F aluminum crochet hook, or size required for gauge

Size 18 tapestry needle

Straight pins

GAUGE:

4 fans = 5 1/2"

10 rows = 4"

Crochet Instructions

CENTER

Ch 204 loosely.

Row 1 (right side): Sc in 2nd ch from hook, sk next 2 chs, in next ch work (dc, ch 1, dc, ch 1, dc): fan made; sk next 2 chs, sc in next ch, * ch 3, sc in next ch, sk next 2 chs, in next ch work (dc, ch 1, dc, ch 1, dc): fan made; sk next 2 chs, sc in next ch; rep from * across: 29 fans; ch 7 (counts as a trc and a ch-3 lp on following rows), turn.

Row 2: * In 2nd dc of next fan work (sc, ch 3, sc), ch 3, dc in next ch-3 lp, ch 3; rep from * across to last fan; in 2nd dc of next fan work (sc, ch 3, sc), ch 3, trc in next sc; ch 1, turn.

Row 3: Sc in next trc, * work fan in next ch-3 lp, in next dc work (sc, ch 3, sc); rep from * across to last ch-3 lp; work fan in next ch-3 lp, sc in next trc: 28 ch-3 lps; ch 7, turn.

Rep Rows 2 and 3 until Center measures about 40". At end of last row, ch 1, turn.

EDGING:

Foundation Rnd: Work 197 sc evenly spaced across top edge to next corner; 2 sc in corner; work 197 sc evenly spaced along next side to next corner; 2 sc in corner; working in unused lps of beg ch, work 197 sc evenly spaced across lower edge to next corner; 2 sc in next corner; work 197 sc evenly spaced along next side; 2 sc in next corner; join in first sc: 796 sc. Finish off and weave in ends.

Hold Center upside down and mark 173rd sc on lower edge of foundation rnd. Set aside.

BORDER

Ch 32 loosely.

Row 1: Sc in 2nd ch from hook and in next 2 chs; (ch 5, sk next 4 chs, sc in next ch) 5 times; ch 5, sk next 2 chs, in next ch work (3 dc, ch 2, 3 dc): shell made: 6 ch-5 lps; ch 5, turn.

Row 2 (right side): In ch-2 sp of next shell work shell: shell in shell made; ch 5, sk next lp, in next lp work (dc, ch 6, dc), ch 5, sk next lp, shell in next lp, ch 5, (sc in next lp, ch 5) twice; sl st in next 3 sc; ch 9, turn.

Row 3: (Sc in next lp, ch 5) twice; sk next lp, shell in next shell, ch 4, sk next lp, 14 trc in next ch-6 lp, ch 4, sk next lp, shell in next shell; ch 5, turn.

Row 4: Shell in next shell, ch 4, sk next ch-4 lp, sc in next 14 trc, ch 4, sk next ch-4 lp, shell in next shell, ch 5, (sc in next ch-5 lp, ch 5) twice; sk next 2 chs of next lp, sc in next 3 chs of same lp; ch 9, turn.

Row 5: (Sc in next lp, ch 5) 3 times; shell in next shell, ch 5, sk next lp and next sc, sc in next 12 sc, ch 5, sk next sc and next lp, shell in next shell; ch 5, turn.

Row 6: Shell in next shell, ch 5, sk next lp and next sc, sc in next 10 sc, ch 5, sk next sc and next lp, shell in next shell,

(continued)

ch 5, (sc in next lp, ch 5) 3 times; sk next 2 chs of next lp, sc in next 3 chs of same lp; ch 9, turn.

Row 7: (Sc in next lp, ch 5) 4 times; shell in next shell, ch 5, sk next lp and next sc, sc in next 8 sc, ch 5, sk next sc and next lp, shell in next shell; ch 5, turn.

Row 8: Shell in next shell, ch 5, sk next lp and next sc, sc in next 6 sc, ch 5, sk next sc and next lp, shell in next shell, ch 5, (sc in next lp, ch 5) 4 times; sk next 2 chs of next lp, sc in next 3 chs of same lp; ch 9, turn.

Row 9: (Sc in next lp, ch 5) 5 times; shell in next shell, ch 5, sk next lp and next sc, sc in next 4 sc, ch 5, sk next sc and next lp, shell in next shell; ch 5, turn.

Row 10: Shell in next shell, ch 5, sk next lp and next sc, sc in next 2 sc, ch 5, sk next sc and next lp, shell in next shell, ch 5, (sc in next lp, ch 5) 5 times; sk next 2 chs of next lp, sc in next 3 chs of same lp; ch 9, turn.

Row 11: (Sc in next lp, ch 5) 6 times; shell in next shell, sk next lp, next 2 sc, and next lp; sc in next shell; ch 5, turn.

Row 12: Shell in next shell, ch 5, sk next lp, in next lp work (dc, ch 6, dc); ch 5, sk next lp, shell in next lp, ch 5, (sc in next lp, ch 5) twice; sk next 2 chs of next lp, sc in next 3 chs of same lp; ch 9, turn.

Rows 13 through 72: Rep Rows 3 through 12 in sequence 6 times.

Rows 73 through 76: Rep Rows 3 through 6. At end of Row 76, ch 8, turn.

Row 77: Rep Row 7.

Row 78: Rep Row 8, ending ch 8, turn.

Row 79: Rep Row 9.

Row 80: Rep Row 10, ending ch 8, turn.

Row 81: Rep Row 11.

Row 82: Rep Row 12, ending ch 8, turn.

Row 83: Rep Row 3.

Row 84: Rep Row 4, ending ch 7, turn.

Row 85: Rep Row 5.

Row 86: Rep Row 6, ending ch 7, turn.

Row 87: Rep Row 7.

Row 88: Rep Row 8, ending ch 7, turn.

Row 89: Rep Row 9.

Row 90: Rep Row 10, ending ch 7, turn.

Row 91: Rep Row 11.

Row 92: Sk next sc, sc in next shell, ch 5, (sc in next lp, ch 5) 6 times; sk next 2 chs of next lp, sc in next 3 chs; ch 6, turn.

Row 93: Sk next 3 sc, sc in next lp, (ch 5, sc in next lp) 7 times; ch 5, turn.

Row 94: Sk next sc, sc in next lp, (ch 5, sc in next lp) 6 times; ch 5, turn.

Rows 95 through 97: Rep Row 94.

Row 98: Sk next sc, (sc in next lp, ch 5) 7 times; working along side edge, sc in next lp, ch 5, sk next lp: corner made sk next 2 chs of next lp, sc in next 3 chs; ch 6, turn.

Row 99: Sk next 3 sc, sc in next lp, (ch 5, sc in next lp) 6 times; ch 5, turn.

Row 100: Sk next sc, shell in next lp, ch 5, sk next lp, in next lp work (dc, ch 6, dc), ch 5, sk next lp, shell in next lp, ch 5, sc in next lp, ch 5, sk next 2 chs of next lp, sc in next 3 chs; ch 6, turn.

Row 101: Sk next 3 sc, (sc in next lp, ch 5) twice; shell in next shell, ch 4, 14 trc in next ch-6 lp, ch 4, shell in next shell; ch 5, turn.